**EXPLORATIONS**

# THE ENDURANCE EXPEDITION

BY DALTON RAINS

WWW.APEXEDITIONS.COM

Copyright © 2025 by Apex Editions, Mendota Heights, MN 55120. All rights reserved. No part of this book may be reproduced or utilized in any form or by any means without written permission from the publisher.

Apex is distributed by North Star Editions:
sales@northstareditions.com | 888-417-0195

Produced for Apex by Red Line Editorial.

Photographs ©: Science Source, cover; Frank Hurley/Scott Polar Research Institute/University of Cambridge/Hulton Archive/Getty Images, 1, 8–9, 10–11, 26–27; Hulton Deutsch/Corbis Historical/Getty Images, 4–5; CBW/Alamy, 6–7, 29; PA Images/Getty Images, 12–13; Shutterstock Images, 14, 16–17, 22–23; PA Images/Alamy, 18; iStockphoto, 19, 20–21, 25; Smith Archive/Alamy, 24

Library of Congress Control Number: 2024940536

**ISBN**
979-8-89250-328-0 (hardcover)
979-8-89250-366-2 (paperback)
979-8-89250-439-3 (ebook pdf)
979-8-89250-404-1 (hosted ebook)

Printed in the United States of America
Mankato, MN
012025

## NOTE TO PARENTS AND EDUCATORS

Apex books are designed to build literacy skills in striving readers. Exciting, high-interest content attracts and holds readers' attention. The text is carefully leveled to allow students to achieve success quickly. Additional features, such as bolded glossary words for difficult terms, help build comprehension.

## CHAPTER 1
### TOWARD ANTARCTICA 4

## CHAPTER 2
### DRIFTING 10

## CHAPTER 3
### FINDING HELP 16

## CHAPTER 4
### RESCUE 22

**COMPREHENSION QUESTIONS • 28**
**GLOSSARY • 30**
**TO LEARN MORE • 31**
**ABOUT THE AUTHOR • 31**
**INDEX • 32**

CHAPTER 1

# TOWARD ANTARCTICA

In August 1914, the *Endurance* set sail from England. The ship was headed to Antarctica. Ernest Shackleton led its crew. They planned to **trek** across the **continent**.

Ernest Shackleton (front) sailed to Antarctica three times in the 1900s.

The crew reached South Georgia in November. Next, they had to cross the Weddell Sea. Thick **pack ice** filled the water. The ship began sailing through the ice in December.

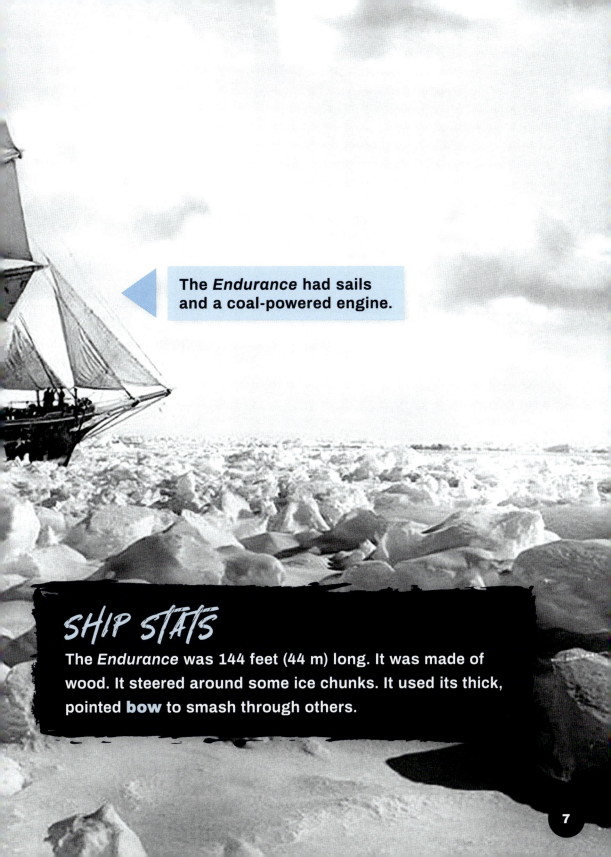

The *Endurance* had sails and a coal-powered engine.

## SHIP STATS

The *Endurance* was 144 feet (44 m) long. It was made of wood. It steered around some ice chunks. It used its thick, pointed **bow** to smash through others.

▲ Crews tried to break up the ice. But the seawater was so cold that it just refroze.

On January 18, the *Endurance* got stuck. By the next morning, the ship was completely trapped in ice.

**FAST FACT**
The Endurance was one day from reaching Antarctica's coast when it got stuck.

**CHAPTER 2**

# DRIFTING

The *Endurance* stayed trapped for months. It slowly drifted north. The crew faced **blizzards** and freezing cold.

The *Endurance* stayed stuck in the ice all winter. In Antarctica, this season lasts from March to October.

More trouble came in October 1915. Ice damaged the *Endurance*. The crew had to **abandon** the ship. They built a camp on the floating ice. The ship sank on November 21.

### SLED DOGS

The crew brought more than 60 dogs on the trip. The dogs were supposed to pull sleds. When the ship got stuck, crew members built igloos for the dogs to live in.

The crew used wood from the ship to build a camp on the ice.

The crew drifted for five more months. Then the ice began to **thaw**. On April 9, 1916, the men boarded three lifeboats. They sailed toward Elephant Island. Seven days later, they landed.

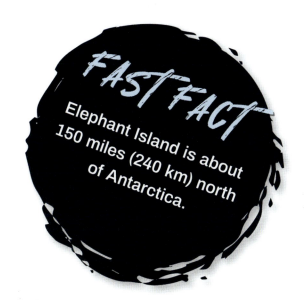

FAST FACT
Elephant Island is about 150 miles (240 km) north of Antarctica.

**Rock and ice cover most of Elephant Island. No people live there.**

CHAPTER 3

# FINDING HELP

Shackleton knew rescue was unlikely. So, he decided to go find help. He picked five men to go with him. The rest of the crew stayed behind.

On Elephant Island, the crew camped at Point Wild. This place was named after Frank Wild, who found it.

**Shackleton's group used the *James Caird*. This lifeboat was just 22.5 feet (6.9 m) long.**

Shackleton's small group left Elephant Island on April 24. They sailed toward South Georgia. Strong winds and storms battered their tiny boat. But the men landed safely on May 10.

## NO MISTAKES

Shackleton's group used a **sextant** to **navigate**. South Georgia was 800 miles (1,290 km) away. Even a small mistake would have made them miss it.

A sextant needs clear skies to work. The men used it just four times during their journey.

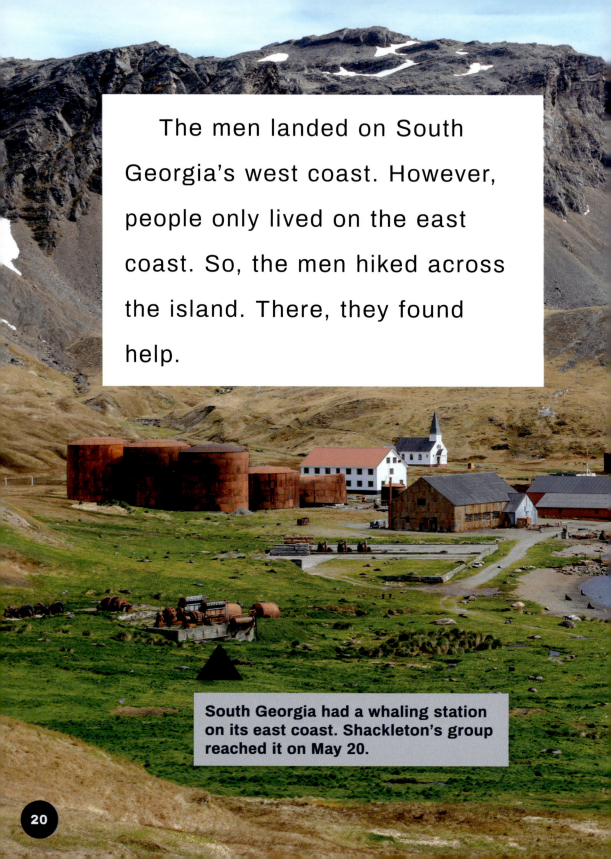

The men landed on South Georgia's west coast. However, people only lived on the east coast. So, the men hiked across the island. There, they found help.

**South Georgia had a whaling station on its east coast. Shackleton's group reached it on May 20.**

## FAST FACT

The men hiked for 36 hours without stopping. They crossed 22 miles (35 km) of mountains.

# CHAPTER 4

# RESCUE

**N**ext, Shackleton tried to return to Elephant Island in a larger ship. He tried three times. Each time, ice or bad weather blocked his route.

Meanwhile, the men on Elephant Island waited. They set up a camp. They faced many days of darkness and cold.

The crew on Elephant Island used upside-down boats as a hut.

**The men on Elephant Island tried to hunt seals and other animals. But they often had very little food.**

## ON THE ISLAND

Frank Wild led the group on Elephant Island. The men hunted penguins and seals each day. At night, they passed the time by singing.

In August 1916, Shackleton tried a fourth time. This time, he succeeded. He reached Elephant Island on August 30. Then he brought everyone back to England.

**The crew survived for four and a half months on Elephant Island.**

**FAST FACT**

Shackleton's entire crew made it back to England. Not one person died.

# COMPREHENSION QUESTIONS

*Write your answers on a separate piece of paper.*

**1.** Write a few sentences describing the main ideas of Chapter 3.

**2.** Would you have wanted to be part of the group that sailed to South Georgia or the group that stayed on Elephant Island? Why?

**3.** How far did Shackleton sail from Elephant Island to South Georgia?

    **A.** 22 miles (35 km)
    **B.** 150 miles (240 km)
    **C.** 800 miles (1,290 km)

**4.** When did Shackleton's crew first land on Elephant Island?

    **A.** April 9, 1916
    **B.** April 16, 1916
    **C.** August 30, 1916

**5.** What does **route** mean in this book?

*Next, Shackleton tried to return to Elephant Island in a larger ship. He tried three times. Each time, ice or bad weather blocked his **route**.*

   **A.** the way someone talks
   **B.** the way to get somewhere
   **C.** a way to stop moving

**6.** What does **succeeded** mean in this book?

*This time, he **succeeded**. He reached Elephant Island on August 30.*

   **A.** sank into the ocean
   **B.** failed to reach a place
   **C.** did what was planned

*Answer key on page 32.*

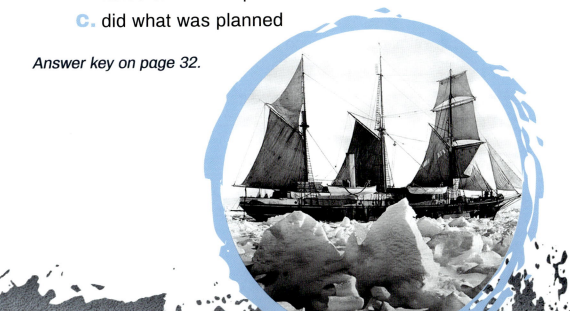

# GLOSSARY

**abandon**

To leave something behind.

**blizzards**

Snowstorms with strong winds.

**bow**

The front part of a ship.

**continent**

One of the seven large pieces of land on Earth.

**navigate**

To find the right way to go when traveling.

**pack ice**

Sea ice that moves around and is not connected to land.

**sextant**

A tool that allows people to use stars to find their way.

**thaw**

To melt or become soft.

**trek**

To make a long journey across land, often on foot.

# TO LEARN MORE

## BOOKS

Morey, Allan. *Exploring Antarctica*. Minneapolis: Bellwether Media, 2023.

Parkin, Michelle. *Southern Ocean Shipwrecks*. Minneapolis: Jump!, 2024.

Rains, Dalton. *Antarctic Scientists*. Mendota Heights, MN: Apex Editions, 2024.

## ONLINE RESOURCES

Visit **www.apexeditions.com** to find links and resources related to this title.

## ABOUT THE AUTHOR

Dalton Rains is an author and editor from Saint Paul, Minnesota.

# INDEX

### A
Antarctica, 4, 9, 15

### C
camp, 12, 24

### D
dogs, 12
drifting, 10, 15

### E
Elephant Island, 15, 18, 22, 24–26
*Endurance*, 4, 6–9, 12
England, 4, 26–27

### H
hunting, 25

### I
ice, 6–8, 12, 15, 22

### L
lifeboats, 15

### S
Shackleton, Ernest, 4, 16, 18–19, 22, 26–27
South Georgia, 6, 18–20

### W
Weddell Sea, 6
Wild, Frank, 25

**ANSWER KEY:**
1. Answers will vary; 2. Answers will vary; 3. C; 4. B; 5. B; 6. C